PIERRE PAULIN

© 2004 Assouline Publishing for the present edition
601 West 26th Street, 18th floor
New York, NY 10001, USA
Tel.: 212 989-6810   Fax: 212 647-0005
www.assouline.com

First published by Editions Assouline, Paris, France.

Translated from the French by David Wharry.

Color separation: Gravor (Switzerland)
Printed in France by *Partenaires-Livres*® (JL)

ISBN: 2 84323 567 7

PIERRE PAULIN

ÉLISABETH VÉDRENNE

ASSOULINE

His sensual and elegant chairs are known around the world and have become classics. His spirit and forms have guided, and continue to inspire, many contemporary international designers in the 21st century. His key works are in the world's greatest museums. But who is Pierre Paulin?

A frustrated artist

Pierre Paulin was born in Paris in 1927, to a French dentist and a German-Swiss mother, for whom order and discipline was important. His mother left an enduring mark on her son, and the tense family atmosphere—his infancy living from hand to mouth in Paris's Bastille quarter and childhood in Laon, a drab dormitory town for railroad workers in the middle of France's northern plain—left him with bad memories. The only escape was holidays in the Swiss mountains, which have remained a place of refuge for him. Paulin now lives in the Cévennes region in southern France.

For a long time, Paulin was shy and reserved, and like many loners, he was a dreamer. His uncle Georges Paulin, an automobile-designer, was the young Paulin's hero. Georges was the designer of a Bentley Streamline and a Peugeot convertible. A Swiss great uncle, a sculptor, also clearly influenced him. Suitably inspired, Paulin went to mould clay at Vallauris, a pottery region in south-eastern France, and then carve stone near Beaune. Yet his destiny was changed by an accident. During a fight, he severed a nerve in his hand ensuring he would never become a sculptor. Yet Paulin definitely had an artistic sensibility; he was clever with his hands and keen to get started, so he decided upon his designer uncle's career. In 1951, Paris was the only place to be, and Paulin was admitted to the École Camondo. The training, however, bored him, although he did learn the lexicon of French classical furniture styles, elements which have occasionally resurfaced in his work. One of his teachers, the decorator Maxime Old, recognized Paulin's talent and advised him to join Marcel Gascoin's design team upon leaving the school. Gascoin's "modern" spirit suited him better. In France at the time everything that wasn't ancient was "modern," and the term "contemporary" was not yet used. Paulin's inevitable rise had begun.

A young functionalist

During Paulin's short stay at Marcel Gascoin's studio, he worked with Pierre Guariche and Michel Mortier and discovered the new Scandinavian designers. Paulin learned quickly and soon left for

Scandinavia to learn more about their austere simplicity tempered by a love of light, nature, and honey-colored wood. These sparsely populated countries shared a profound sense of community, which led to the emergence of an extremely functional design based on the same rationalism and common sense that molded traditional Scandinavian forms. There, Paulin discovered the work of "organic modernist" Alvar Aalto. Aalto succeeded in softening an ideology similar to the great Bauhaus modernists; his serene, gently undulating plywood forms had none of their brutality. Paulin was completely won over.

Briefly working at the Galeries Lafayette design studio, Paulin discovered American designer Charles Eames's work in the magazine *Interiors*. He became an enthusiast, steeping himself in Eames's work and drawing great inspiration from his pragmatic genius. Indeed, this was a time of influences. Paulin also admired Georges Nelson, whom he found more sensitive and a kindred spirit. The oyster chair he designed for Artifort was critiqued by some for "over-assimilating" Nelson's Coconut chair. Paulin has never denied his influences, though he insists that he first saw Nelson's chair after he'd designed his own. He was, in fact, envious of the American designers who worked for furniture firms such as the Herman Miller Furniture Company and Knoll Associates, which still fascinates him today.

Paulin dreamed of working in their stimulating environment. This didn't prevent him from launching his own line, at 26, with his father as manufacturer, and exhibiting a project at the Salon des Arts Ménagers in 1953. It was an instant success, and immediately made the cover of *La Maison Française* magazine! From 1953 to

1967 he worked on a furniture series for Thonet France, where he learned that design also meant being flexible, respecting the clients' specifications, working in a group project, and having to make a profit. During this time he designed his most beautiful early chairs, produced by Meubles TV in 1954. Lightness, balance, sensuality—the Paulin style was born. The seat: a simple ring formed by four pieces of leather sewn together and stretched around a central hole; the base: two folded stainless-steel squares held together by rings. The result: a comfortable, ultra-simple, airy chair. Similar chairs followed, manufactured by Artifort, one bag-shaped, in chromed steel and leather; the other consisting of two separate leather bands on a beautiful, very light, geometric frame (1963), which Artifort is now producing again (no. 675).

The glorious sixties

Like many postwar "young Turks," Paulin assimilated the free-form concept in the late fifties. Charles Eames' and Elio Saarinen's shell chairs and Noguchi's and Perriand's puddle and bean-shaped tables quickly led him to favor sinuous lines and curves. Paulin was one of the last "moderns" to serve up rigor in an "organic" sauce, as the great Finnish designer Alvar Aalto did in the thirties. Paulin's furniture softened, began to undulate, took on more natural forms, and, ever-rational, banished exaltation and exaggeration.

In 1958, Harry Wagemans, chief executive of the Dutch firm Artifort, offered him financial backing and a free hand. At last, his ideas could be put into practice. He could finally experiment, transpose, compare, synthesize, carry out tests—be the creative link in the design chain. Paulin was confident enough to innovate both formally and in his use of materials; to take the realization and production of a piece of furniture through to completion. He exploited advances in industrial techniques to their maximum, including fully utilizing new plastics. Inspired by metal-frame and webbed automobile seats, he used Pirelli rubber and foam rubber covered with elasticized jersey fabric. Softening angles and lines became the credo.

Paulin became part of the zeitgeist, and drew upon the contemporary ideas which affected everyone differently. The sixties were the Pop years and Paulin has been too easily classified as a product of Pop. He denied this label, and was not concerned with Pop in the strictest sense of the word, which has come to define a precise artistic movement. Paulin was a designer of his time. Many of his works have become icons of the carefree, upbeat, and prosperous years now definitively labeled Pop—and they were popular.

The french exception

In 1960, the French concept of "design" was vague. The new sense of the word was unclear. Although "industrial draftsmen" had begun to appear, like the Gascoin studio which specialized in storage furniture, they were slow to launch into the furniture market. Traditionally, furniture design was then either the domain of decorators-cum-interior designers, or the work of a few avant-garde architects and wayward engineers. There was no company design culture, and design research teams working with industry were rare—unlike in the United States and Scandinavia, or in Italy, where a new generation of "Made in Italy" products were already being developed.

France lagged behind, and found it hard to catch up. Many designer precursors didn't survive and were only recognized internationally much later. It took a lot of courage to be a furniture designer or manufacturer in France in the fifties and sixties. The few who managed to persevere found it hard to express their talents and struggled. Some, concerned themselves with the visual quality of products, like Raymond Loewy in the United States. These were isolated successes, though, and many failed. There was no shortage of passion or ideas among French furniture manufacturers, just one missing link—the interest and curiosity of industrialists, retailers, and advertising agencies. Paulin forged his career in this design desert. Beginning as an obstacle course in France, but later becoming easier with the opportunity of working abroad, international recognition in the United States and Japan, and finally, acclaim after twenty years of difficulty.

The art of relaxation

With hindsight, it seems that everybody during that energetic era just wanted to lounge around. It is striking how many "relaxed" chairs Paulin designed for Artifort in those dynamic years between 1959 and 1974. Is that really what people did: sit down, lie down, rest, and sleep? Was *homo sapiens* turning into *"homo sedens"* and *"homo ludens?"* Relaxation, anyway, became an art form, providing Paulin with the perfect opportunity to create a vast family of forms.

His chairs were rounded, well-padded, but never as buxom as the ideologically unabashed UP chair series in expanded polyurethane covered with stretch fabric which Gaetano Pesce designed in 1969. Paulin never theorized or empathized.

They were organic but never vulgar. It is hard to imagine Paulin accepting the Airborne furniture advertisement with its huge poster covered with naked buttocks, or Roger Tallon's Cryptogame stools, photographed with a nude woman sitting on them. These close to the ground chairs were not for sprawling out on but reclining comfortably on: to relax without being sloppy. Even his Tongue chair has poise. There was no limpness with Paulin, just comfort. Indeed, he held the minority view. Even his brilliant friend Verner Panton subjected the body to acrobatic contortions. There were no genuinely ergonomic chairs at that time; above all, forms had to be daring.

Inspired by the forms of the body and its metaphors, by contrast, Paulin's chairs were always elegant, not espousing the skeleton, but evoking its presence. Not the body itself but the idea of its "liberation." A chair should make one feel like moving, sitting in a thousand different ways, stretching, dreaming, playing the guitar, talking. It should not be a straitjacket holding you in place. The backside prefers to sit in the middle of a large circle, a sun or a moon, preferably padded, but it's also comfortable in steel mesh, sticks, or plastic! It was invention that counted. True comfort was neither a Pop nor Hippy priority. One of the few to consider this was Charles Eames, whose Lounge chair was the most comfortable chair of its time and a godsend to psychoanalysts.

Sixties' chairs dreamed of becoming hammocks, being playful and changing into beds. They were a natural, late evolution of the traditional chaise lounge, which Paulin took one step further with one of his most beautiful designs, the *Déclive*, a new form of "sleeper" chair he invented (like a flying carpet that can be shaped and transformed into a modern, canopied four-poster bed). The prototype, comprising foam-padded slats assembled on an articulated aluminum frame, was made by Mobilier National in 1968, but has sadly never been produced. Another marvel of calligraphic elegance was his 1968 "back-to-back" bench prototype for the Musée du Louvre. His more revolutionary hybrid *tapis-séjour*, a Western version of the Japanese *tatami* that spreads out over the floor, has also never been produced. Paulin experimented for a long time with a beige prototype, the only version ever built, in his Paris home. A futurist vision of a magical oriental carpet, its four corners, raised in triangles supported by squares, form backs to lean against.

The plastic-elastic-artistic years

These chairs seek reincarnation as the universal "shell," as if we need protection like an unborn child. The spherical shell had already been formulated by the Danish designer Jacobsen in his Egg chair and radicalized by the Finn Eero Aarnio in Pastili, his giant, hollowed-out pouf in fiberglass-reinforced polyester, polished and hard as a pebble, and his 1963 capsule-shaped Ball armchair that could be suspended from the ceiling (Bubble chair) like a pod. Now it grew lighter and looser. It unfolded into a corolla and took on a classical form in the Tulip chairs Eero Saarinen designed for Knoll. There is one major difference with Paulin, though: his open-shell chairs rarely come in rigid fiberglass, the material that enabled single-piece furniture. His structures had a rounded, "containing" form like a nest, cupped palm, crown, or flower, but they had a metal structure with foam-padded webbing. Paulin's forms suggest movement; their texture suggests flesh. Just consider the voluptuous circumvolutions of his Ribbon chair or the rounded and welcoming nature of his celebrated Mushroom chair, a highly successful metamorphosis of the 19th-century squat armchair, that Paulin himself considers his most accomplished design.

The skin interested him as much as the body. Curvaceous women in swimsuits gave him the idea of enveloping his chairs in soft, figure-hugging stretch covers. The technique was already being used, but he had the innovative idea of sheathing upholstery in a newly invented material, elasticized jersey. Paulin was the first designer to "dress" his chairs in the same fabric as the miniskirts of Yves Saint Laurent and Pierre Cardin. Artifort adopted elasticized jersey as a furnishing fabric, using designs more Op than Pop by great textile designers such as Jack Lenor Larsen.

Jersey was particularly flexible and resistant, and it hugged and maintained the foam like sheath, containing it and compressing without wrinkles or creases. This enabled Paulin to further simplify and eliminate, to retain only what was necessary. These chairs seemed to have been sculpted and curl up in space.

Paulin's colors were vitamin-packed, full of pep: bright green, yellow, orange, Schiaperelli's "shocking" pink, violet, poppy red, and deep sky blue. Paulin and Verner Panton (whose colors were more eclectic), were the only designers to use so many colors. The man who loved only immaculate white and "Paulin blue" proved he could cater to contemporary young consumers' tastes. His favorite color was more intimate: a pale blue, sometimes like a radiant sky, sometimes melancholy and gray-tinted like the sky blue of French soldiers' uniforms in World War One. Paulin had no time for the "suaveness" he said was typical of the time when Courrèges's pastel-colored models were like young girls gone to seed, all "vinyl and daisy." Nor did he like the "shapeless," like the famous Sacco chair, whose pellet-filled envelope perfectly weds the body's forms, and also causes back problems.

The Paulin style

Paulin furniture is easily recognizable: rational, elegantly drawn, full of charm, humor, and spirit, beautifully finished with carefully thought-out attention to detail. His forms are sensual and restrained, warm and rigorous. They have character and posture, they are radiant and light, and in every sense of the word they assert themselves harmoniously. In short, they are graceful.

A Paulin chair has characteristic proportions. It is always balanced and precise. He studied the characteristics of modular furniture, which was common at the time, and befitted the social culture.

His undulating ABCD sofa was not a single piece but an assembly of juxtaposed, foam-packed, stretch-covered shells (1968, Artifort). His modular chairs can be placed alone or end to end to create long serpentine couches in offices or public places. But Paulin abhorred heaviness, folds, thick wrinkles in leather, anything imposing, massive, or exhibitionist.

Some called his work respectable upper middle class; others regarded it as the epitome of universal elegance. The plain sofa had become too bourgeois; the never-ending modular couch was the latest fashion. Marco Zanuso had already designed his seminal Lombrico sofa in 1966—polyester reinforced with fiberglass and foam upholstery covered with wool fabric. It is still produced by B&B Italia.

Paulin took the idea further in 1970 with Amphis for Mobilier National. He placed large modules end to end, so that their articulated structure, which could snake around at will placed directly on the new and essential element of interior decoration, the wall-to-wall carpet (Paulin preferred the white woolen rug), had complete mobility. The three sausage components on metal frames could be assembled in different color combinations: there was a Neapolitan slice version, and Habitat relaunched the red-and-white version in 1998. A three-color blue-white-red version was chosen for the French pavilion at the 1970 Osaka Universal Exposition, and an all-red version was ordered for the lobby of the Hotel Nikko, Paris, in 1976.

The Paulin style? The quintessence of voluptuous sobriety.

The poetics of space

Pierre Paulin has often said he would have wanted to be an architect. Indeed, he designed his own house. Yet, if his chairs are so at home in any space, it's because he is passionately interested in spatial arrangements. This taste was forged in the fifties by designing the stands at numerous salons: the Salon des Arts Ménagers, the Salon de l'Automobile, as well as exhibitions, the Maison de la Télévision, the Maison de la Radio, hotels, etc. The concept of concealing lighting behind fabric stretched on metal frames, a technique he continues to use, also began this way. Fabric is often used to hide ugly-looking things, but Paulin saw it as a dream, an embellishment, as purity. This was his idealistic side. He claims not to be interested in fabric, yet his use of it became a hallmark.

Jersey sheathed his seats, fabric covered the walls, absorbed the light. On exhibition stands, in homes and offices, or in President Pompidou's private apartment in the Elysée Palace, Paulin conceived space as a superb, malleable bubble. He drew on his memories of oriental architecture, which he loved to see stripped of its gilding. He magnified this by using monastic white and softened it with filtered lighting. This was a sign of his admiration for Japan, and the way light is filtered through screens or paper, as in Noguchi's work.

Paulin created an atmosphere of diffuse clarity. Blessed with the gift of enlarging space by reducing it, he remodeled it using snowy, supple velum-like fabrics whose texture feels like a second skin. He loved to create the impression of movement and invented systems to make the fabric swell, tremble, undulate, and breathe like a sail. Gothic grottos with luminous stalactites, Romanesque-style vaults, igloos, and Bedouin tents with languid, fluid ceilings were just some of the surfaces he created.

Marc Bohan's studio and Christian Dior's offices were designed by Paulin in 1967, all-white rooms lit by split lamps that looked like eyes. For the Pompidous in 1971, it was beige on Mme. Claude Pompidou's wishes, as her husband would have preferred "his" blue. The ceilings were lowered to hide the 19th-century wood paneling behind screens of elasticized fabric, he integrated the seating into the architecture, eliminated doors, and closed the windows of the smoking room, which were transformed into a surreal cocoon. The smoked-glass tables in the dining room were lit from beneath, and he transformed the ceiling into a luminous, curved vault with a gigantic chandelier made of glass rods. The small drawing room was turned into a communicant's candy box, lit by round wall lamps that created halos on the padded walls, and he placed a low, round, flower-shaped table in the center of the room.

Paulin lamps

People often talk about Paulin's lighting, but rarely about his lamps. They are few and grand in style, like those at the Elysée Palace which can be transformed into standard lamps with round moonlike tops, or other standard lamps that are merely vertical halogen tubes. The wall lamps are made of bouquets of wires ending in tiny light bulbs or bunches of small mushroom heads pointing downward, or candle-ends turned upward (Maison de la Radio,

1961; Salon des Artistes Décorateurs, Grand Palais, 1963), or they could reach down from the ceiling, sometimes very low, like meteorites or shooting stars.

They were poetic, with Paulin once again ahead of his time. It is less well known, though, that he created flower-shaped lamps, the kind of naive flowers common in Pop imagery (Andy Warhol, Marimekko), with large petals, wide open or tightly shut at the end of articulated stems. These lamps were sometimes painted white, to heighten the source of light, preferably indirect, or sometimes red, and most of them were made in Pierre Disderot's workshop at Cachan, or by Jacques Vidal.

It's still striking to see how fresh and fashionable these lamps still are, and to realize how much Paulin's designs have been studied, analyzed, digested, assimilated, even copied. These "imitations," which are considered classic and contemporary, are reusing forms and a creative spirit that is thirty or forty years old.

Paulin is scathing on this subject, labeling several famous designers as "necrophagous" and "tomb-pillagers." He drew inspiration from his immediate elders, but too many young designers shamelessly devour their grandparents. The outcome remains uncertain.

The design studio years

The ensuing years were less flamboyant and, seemingly, less contradictory. Paulin grew tired of being internationally famous, while being barely recognized by his French peers. His eclecticism worked against him: he was considered too subservient to institutions and presidential commissions; labeled as Pompidou's decorator; and categorized as an elitist artist who worked for the Mobilier National. Paulin's professionalism, corporate experience, functionalist ideals, and interest in community were unfairly brushed aside. People forgot he was one of the last true modernists. The times had changed: bright colors disappeared, black-and-white, angular rationalism came back in force, chic high-tech aesthetics replaced naive optimism. The seventies, the decade of the oil crisis, were more austere. In 1975, Paulin joined his wife, Maïa Wodzislawska, at the agency she had created, which they renamed AD/SA. He worked there for twenty years, and was joined by Roger Tallon. Responsible for the visual identity of their products and logos, Paulin worked with French firms on purely industrial projects, including irons (the Jetline 10) and electric razors for Calor, stackable garden chairs in injected plastic, reminiscent of Thonet's chairs for Allinert, etc. Other clients included Sommer, Thomson, Villeroy & Bosch, Citroën, and the SNCF. Paulin was back in the fold, working in teams, executing commissions.

Frustration, however, increased in the early eighties. Paulin's desire for controversy arose, as did his so-called taste for luxury: the most luxurious kind, unique and simple. He grew tired yet fascinated by the acclaim granted a new generation of designers, who advocated a design revolution: a total break with the constraints of modernism and functionalism, which they regarded as sterile and lacking inventiveness. These rebels, mainly Italian (Memphis), English, American, and Spanish, famously declared new movements such as postmodernism, new-baroque, and so on. Paulin, himself a radical, was about to begin a strange adventure of his own.

A time for adventure

With a mischievous hint, and a blend of craftiness and naivete, Paulin amused himself by designing a collection of chairs and a few small desks, "flitting from idea to idea in the byways of the past." It was like a voyage to Cythera, where he could practice his scales and exercise his style with all the sparkling lightness he is known for.

As expected, this move was greeted with confusion. Paulin saw himself as "a man of the Enlightenment," no longer capable of inventing, but improvising with great refinement and pleasure, variations on the shapes of chairs in the history of design. Working in wood ("but so did Eames!") with the supremely skilled craftsmen at the Mobilier National, Paulin allowed himself a perverse voluptuousness, one he considered well deserved, happily traversing periods and lightening forms to retain only their substance. He took the curule chair as his starting point, the folding X-shaped chair of Roman money-lenders and consuls became the Savonarola chair in 16th-century Italy, passing by the Ming Dynasty high-backed armchair (the Dane Hans Wegner designed an entire series), and finally ending on chairs partially inspired by Art Deco. Throwing himself wholeheartedly into stylistic affectation, he used red amaranth wood when Sotsass was using imitation, veneering furniture with flecked plastic in Third World colors. Marquetry palm leaves, alveoli for Cathedral, his lacquered metal table with diagonal strut legs... However, what he considered "thumbing his nose at the École Camondo" was badly received, as his writing desks and cabinets broke with the cozy "modern" Paulin image.

It seems Paulin never appears where he's expected. Despite his idolization today, his "cabinetmaker" period is ignored. How will people react to this independent and uncontrollable designer's next furniture collection, which has been made with new materials under great secrecy?

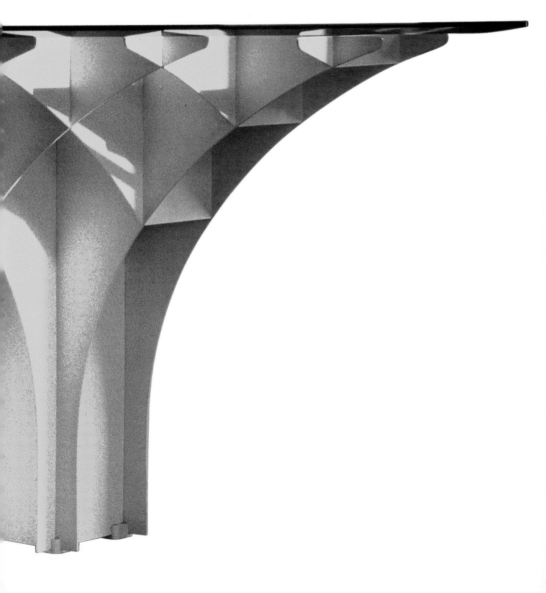

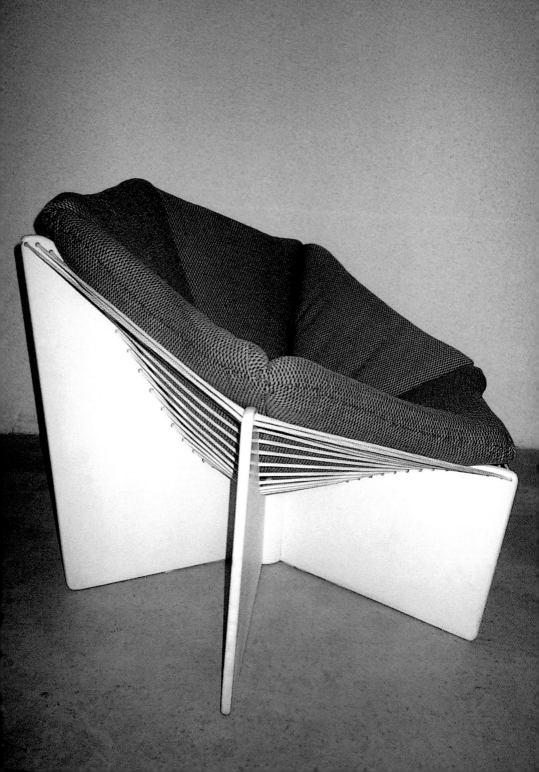

Chronology

1927: Born in Paris on July 29, to a French father and a German-speaking Swiss mother.

1951: Studies at the École Camondo in Paris, works in Marcel Gascoin's studio with Michel Mortier and Pierre Guariche, discovers Scandinavian and American design. Admires Charles Eames, George Nelson, Alexander Girard, and Harry Bertoia, but also Eero Saarinen, Florence Knoll, and Franco Albini.

1953: His first furniture, produced with his father's help and shown in the Foyer d'Aujourd'hui section at the Salon des Arts Ménagers, Paris, is a dazzling media success.
Starts designing for Thonet France.

1957: *French Contemporary Art* exhibition, New York.
Noticed by the Korean Kho Liang Ie, he meets Harry Wagemans, chief executive of the Dutch firm Artifort. Becomes friends with the upholsterer Nico Cilissen, with whom he devises his famous jersey fabric. Artifort is still producing his classic designs today.

1959: Artifort: Mushroom chair no. 560, no legs, sheathed in jersey. Still in production.

1961: All-glass display window for Roche-Bobois, Boulevard Saint-Germain, Paris. Still on view.
Designs the Foyer des Artistes at the Maison de la Radio, Paris.

1963: Designs the hall of the Salon des Artistes Décorateurs, Paris.

1964: Artifort: Tongue chair no. 577, low armless unit chair. Still in production.

1965: Designs the hall of the Buttes-Chaumont TV studios, Paris.
First *tapis-séjour* presented at the Salon des Arts Ménagers, Paris.

1966: Artifort: Ribbon chair no. 582, in the design collections of MoMA, New York, and the Musée National d'Art Moderne-Centre Georges Pompidou, Paris. Still in production.

1968: *Les Assises du siège contemporain*, Musée des Arts Décoratifs, Paris. A seminal exhibition forced to close prematurely due to the May 1968 student uprising.
Begins a long collaboration with Jean Coural at the Mobilier National design studio. Renovation of the Musée du Louvre, Paris, with Monpoix.

1969: The Déclive, prototype by Mobilier National. Paulin donated it and his *tapis-séjour* to the Centre de Création Industrielle-Musée National d'Art Moderne (Centre Georges Pompidou), where there is a room devoted to it.

1970: Amphis sausage sofa, made by Mobilier National for the French Pavilion at the Osaka Universal Exposition, Japan.
Modern Chairs *1918-1970* exhibition, Whitechapel Gallery, London.

1971: *Design français*, first exhibition at the Centre de Création Industrielle (Centre Georges Pompidou), Paris.

1972: Designs President Pompidou's apartments for Mobilier National.

One of the vintage Paulin icons: his 1968 Orange Slice, covered with fabric designed by Jack Lenor Larsen. Artifort.

1975:	Founds the AD/SA agency with his wife, Maïa Wodzislawska, and Marc Lebailly. They are joined later by Roger Tallon and Michel Schreiber. Purely industrial design, for a period of about twenty years.
1976:	Lobby of the Hotel Nikko, Paris.
1983:	Exhibits a collection of furniture in precious woods at the Musée des Arts Décoratifs, Paris. Classically inspired curule chairs and Chinese-style chairs in amaranth wood, marquetry, and caning.
1984:	Designs President Miterrand's office at the Elysée Palace (armchairs, caned desk chair, desk) for Mobilier National.
1985:	Furniture for the Tapestry Room at Paris City Hall.
1987:	Receives the Grand Prix National de Création Industrielle.
1988:	*Les Années Cinquante* exhibition, Centre Georges Pompidou, Paris.
1992:	*Manifeste* exhibition, Centre Georges Pompidou, Paris. Publication of Anne Chapoutot's monograph *Un Univers des Formes* (Editions du May, Paris, out of print).
1995:	Pierre Paulin now lives and works at Saint-Roman-de-Codières in the Gard.
1998:	Habitat's new managing director, English designer Tom Dixon, includes Mushroom and Amphis (under the name Osaka) in the Habitat catalogue.
1999:	Exhibition at the École des Beaux-Arts, Nîmes.
2000:	Retrospective, Centre Culturel Français, Rabat, Morocco. Exhibition, Galerie Alain Gutharc, Paris.
2001:	Retrospective, Galerie De Meron, Paris. The Fonds National d'Art Contemporain (FNAC) buys several chairs. Publication of *Paulin* by Elisabeth Védrenne and Anne-Marie Fèvre (Editions Dis Voir, Paris).
2003:	Opening of the permanent Paulin room at the Musée National d'Art Moderne-Centre Georges Pompidou. Exhibition organized by the gallery Kreo at the MK2 multiplex in the 13th arrondissement, Paris. Works on a collection for the Italian furniture manufacturer Magis.
2004:	Shows at the *Design & Sièges de Collection* exhibition at the Salon du Meuble, Paris. Exhibition of rare pieces from the 1960s and 1970s, Galerie De Meron, Paris.

Pierre Paulin

Ribbon chair no. 582 (1965). Artifort publicity photo. Elasticized fabric designed by Jack Lenor Larsen. White gloss-painted wood base. ©Artifort/All rights reserved.

Groovy chairs no. 598 (1973). Artifort. Tubular structure with horizontal spring, latex foam, jersey cover, protective base rail in anodized aluminum. © Artifort/All rights reserved.

Maison de la Radio, Paris, (1961). The Foyer des Artistes, with chairs, precursors of the Globe armchairs (1957–59), manufactured by Thonet. The low ceiling lights are also by Paulin. © Archives Pierre Paulin/All rights reserved.
Little Globe chair no. 427 (1960). Artifort publicity photo. There is a version with a higher back, *Globe* no. 422, and foot rest no. 421. Beech shell, foam upholstery, aluminum pedestal. © Artifort/All rights reserved.

The red prototype of back-to-back OP-NP (1966-1968). The precursor of the *Déclive*, made at the Mobilier National research and creation studio. Shown at the *Les Assises du Siège Contemporain* exhibition at the Musée des Arts Décoratifs in May 1968. Galerie Kreo Collection. © Marc Domage/Galerie Kreo, Paris/All rights reserved.

The Tulip chairs (1965). Artifort publicity photo. Left, Little Tulip no. 163; middle, with a higher back, Tulip no. 545; right, the foot rest. Artifort. There were many variations. The metal bases here are cruciform; later there would be a single-piece central base. © Artifort/All rights reserved.

The mythical Ribbon chair. Wood base. Produced by Artifort since 1965. Winner of the Chicago Design Award in 1966. In the design collections of MoMA, New York, and the Musée National d'Art Moderne-Centre Georges Pompidou, Paris. © Artifort/All rights reserved.

Amphis sofa system. Foam stretch-covered with jersey fabric. Mobilier National. The red, white, and blue version was shown at the 1970 Osaka Universal Exposition. © Archives Pierre Paulin/All rights reserved.

Amphis sofa, all red, in the lobby of the Hotel Nikko, Paris. The ceiling, entirely constructed out of alveoli, and the incredible "mineral garden" on one side are also by Paulin. © Archives Pierre Paulin/All rights reserved.

The famous Mushroom chairs in two different environments. Left: summer 2003 in the Cévennes. © Photo Philippe Chancel/All rights reserved. Right: Artifort publicity photo, 1960s. © Artifort/All rights reserved.

Mushroom no. 560 (1963). Artifort. Close up from above and behind, on a blue geometric carpet design by Paulin. Tubular structure, foam, and jersey upholstery. © Photo Philippe Chancel/All rights reserved.

No. 300 (1964). Series of single-piece chairs in molded polyurethane. Shown here in white, with the colored jersey-covered trimming. Placed side by side, they form long sofas for public spaces. © Archives Pierre Paulin/All rights reserved.

The Elysée Palace. M. and Mme. Pompidou's library, Paris (1968–1972), methacrylate modules, round smoked-glass tabletop in the foreground. The large round vault, in jersey fabric like the walls, hid the original wood paneling and reduced noise. **Smoking room** in the Elysée Palace, a cocoon with beige elasticized fabric walls incorporating the seats and emphasizing the wood grain lit by the round gloss white lamps. Mobilier National. © Archives Pierre Paulin/All rights reserved.

Cathedral table, 1981. The enormous yet very light base is made of yellow-painted aluminum sheets forming intermeshing diagonal ribs. Glass tabletop. Mobilier National.

Pierre Paulin's loft, rue du Faubourg Saint-Antoine, Paris. In the foreground, no. 675 leather chairs, 1963. In the center, the famous articulated Déclive, now in the Centre Georges Pompidou. The velum ceiling softens the lighting.

Circular seating in the Louvre, Paris (1969–70). Mobilier National, designed specifically for the Grande Galerie of the Louvre.

Top to bottom, left to right: CM 190 chair, molded wood, foam, and steel tubing, Thonet (1954); Oyster chair no. 157, molded wood shell, latex foam, fabric, Artifort (1960); leather chair no. 675, metal wire base, Artifort; Globeo armchair, Thonet (1956–57). Arachnoid armchair, Artifort (1969). Gloss-painted wood base, cord seat covered with a leather cushion. Galerie Kreo Collection.

Wall seat-cum-bed (center, 1953). Meuble TV. Wood-slatted top. Shown in the Foyer d'Aujourd'hui exhibit at the Salon des Arts Ménagers, Paris, and also on the cover of La Maison Française magazine. Right: a lamp from the Mobilier National range, 1970s. On either side, no. 675 leather chairs (1963). Galerie Kreo Collection.

Small wooden desk and chair with steel legs, Thonet (1953). Galerie Kreo Collection.

Showroom, with no. 282, Groovy, Mushroom, Tongue, and Orange Slice chairs. The entire Artifort chair range, with small white tables with similar bases.

Two versions of Tongue chair no. 577 (1967). A sixties icon, now in the design collection of MoMA, New York. An Artifort classic still in production today. Tubular structure, latex foam, and jersey fabric upholstery. © Photos Philippe Chancel.

Folding curule chair in light sycamore wood, canvas back. Also made in amaranth with a leather back. 1982. Paulin. © Photo Philippe Chancel.

White ambience on a Paulin stand at the 1968 Salon des Arts Ménagers. Foreground: prototype of a "tray column," never manufactured. Articulated closed-petal flower lamps. Center: Déclive configured as a bed with dais. © Archives Pierre Paulin/All rights reserved.

Prototype belonging to Pierre Paulin. Metal base forming a kind of very fluid aerial shell; the fabric of the seat and back is the designer's favorite gray-blue. © Photo Philippe Chancel.
1960s publicity photo with Artifort furniture. The woman is sitting in the Globe chair with an aluminum base. In the background, Paulin's Mushroom and Tulip chairs. © Artifort/All rights reserved.

Living room of the Paulins' house in the Cévennes (2003). In the background, on the floor and wall, is the enormous geometric carpet. On the white tiles, low round tables with glass center-flowers and tops, and four immaculate white Tongue chairs. © Photo Philippe Chancel.

Summer 2003, Pierre Paulin at home in the Cézennes. © Photo Philippe Chancel.
The Ribbon chair, red version, in the hall of the Paulin house. © Photo Philippe Chancel.

The author would like to thank Pierre Paulin et Maïa Wodzislawska-Paulin for their patience and for having opened their archives.
The publisher would like to thank for their help: Pierre Paulin et Maïa Wodzislawska-Paulin; Monique Beaumont and Artifort; Didier Krzentowski, the gallery Kreo and Aurélie Julien; the photographer Philippe Chancel.